ZOOM!

Sooner than later, let's GO now!

By: John Mosher & Karen K. Walker, LPC

ZOOM!

ISBN: **0692495029**

ISBN-13: **978-0692495025**

www.createspace.com

www.successfuldirectionsllc.com

www.karenkwalkercounseling.com

Cover design by: Stephen Reed

Dedicated to those who help us find our **ZOOM**!

CONTENTS

FOREWORD

It is with a great desire to clarify, for those who would like to determine their path to success in business and to identify the elements necessary for success that this book was written.

Both authors want to shake the tree and let all the myths fall to the ground and leave only the real reasons for the lack of progress left to be considered.

There will need to be change without it nothing ever really progresses and the reasons are listed for this lack of progress even some regression is possible without first deciding I and we will CHANGE. Let's get started. ZOOM!

INTRODUCTION

In the beginning, there was a beginning, and so here we go. In my years as a business consultant, I have worked all over North America, literally coast to coast, and discovered the biggest difference between cities is really the cost of living. Nothing else is very significant. Everybody thinks his or her area is different in many ways, but the areas really aren't different. Everyone thinks his or her company is different and more troubled than any other, but mostly they aren't. I hedged a little bit there, and the why of that will become evident as we move along.

The many private companies with which I've been involved have taught me so very much. The enlightenment has been blinding at times. I knew the years I had spent with one very successful company gave me great insight as to what success requires of those striving to attain prosperity. I also spent many years attending business conferences where owners of great and would-be great companies gathered.

It became more apparent year after year as to why there were successful and struggling companies, and the divide was pretty much 10 percent successful and 90 percent with a considerable amount of struggle, so off I went to fix things. As a result of this 12-year effort to repair and reorganize corporate systems, I learned so much. I want to share those findings with you. I will not only divulge the key elements of financial success, but also the reason why success does and doesn't happen and why many companies are not able to push concepts to fruition.

John Mosher

My time as a professional counselor with individuals and business men and women, has enlightened me on how many people are stuck in their lives. There appears to be a desire for change, but they lack understanding of how to change. It's like new shoes and old shoes. If you're going to a place where you know you'll have to walk a lot, and you have a choice between wearing your old shoes that have seen their day, or new shoes that aren't broken in yet, most will choose their old shoes.

I believe that is because you know what to expect; you are comfortable with the familiar. This is the same avoidance of change that is apparent in all walks of life. It is what keeps us stuck in business, in relationships, and in stumbling toward but not accomplishing your dreams and desires. It is fear of the unknown. It is fear. Once you have awareness of what holds you back, you will know where to start to get out of your own way.

You have to be willing to put on your new shoes and start walking the next leg of your journey. We want to be part of your journey. We are here to help you get on your path and truly find your way.

Find Your ZOOM.

Karen Walker

1. ZOOM

verb \ˈzüm\

: **to move quickly**

: **to move quickly upward**

: **to increase suddenly**

ZOOM, ZOOM, ZOOM, and ZOOM

So what is "ZOOM"? For our purposes here, ZOOM is getting from where we are to where we want or need to be as quickly as possible by eliminating the barriers to our goals.

To go unfettered in the direction of our goals with dispatch, we must have a very clear plan to execute; otherwise, we could fall off the path with ease. We have to remember that's already our inclination, either because we're really afraid or very easily distracted. That resistance is present in all of us to varying degrees. We can't just dismiss it; we have to move forward in spite of it. Each time we push through the stumbling block, it gets easier.

"The coward dies a thousand deaths, the brave but one."
William Shakespeare

So now having eliminated or at least acknowledged our reluctance to change, we can move forward with creating a plan that involves all the key participants (everybody on board, please). A good solid plan and the ability to be flexible when necessary while staying focused on the goals. No procrastinating. Find your ZOOM, and get going!

"My mission in life is to not merely survive, but to thrive; and to do so with some passion, some compassion, some humor, and some style." Maya Angelou

2. PASSION

noun \ ˈpaSHən

: strong and barely controllable emotion

Passion is the driver of all inspiration. Passion is the stuff of life itself. Grand success, great accomplishments, and the desire to keep going: These are the results of passion. Can you acquire it? Can you develop it? Is it already there?

For the entrepreneur to really keep moving down the path to great success, the passion for developing the entity has to take precedence over the individual elements of the entity. This might sound like a contradiction, but we don't think it really is. The individual elements and -- sometimes, yes – responsibility for and care of the shiny new thing must be put in the proper perspective and even assigned to others. Are you ready to build this grand dream and have the successful business you once envisioned?

We must have a truly focused passion and be disciplined in this effort. We have to be! There'll be plenty of time to dream and explore new opportunities, but we don't want this to impede our forward progress toward the big picture goals that will make so many other adventures possible.

Example: We decide to take on a new management system and we feel that we need to be at the center of this new system's installation and the initial running of the system. When we do this at the expense of the big picture, we lose focus and momentum. In any company, it has been stated that 10% are actively engaged. This 10% wants to see the company blossom and grow, which benefits these employees as well. Then there is 10% that are actively disengaged. They often represent the "cancer" in the corporation. They are not passionate about the organization as a whole, but are predictors of failure. They bring a negative spirit to the organization. Then the remaining 80% tend to be disengaged. They want to punch a clock, collect their pay, and get to the weekend. A successful company will eliminate the actively disengaged and recruit a percentage of the 80% disengaged to bring them into engagement.

Passion is the fuel that ignites your ZOOM. Passion is the intrinsic motivator that gets you out of bed each day. Passion is the difference between a person who simply works at a job and a true entrepreneur. Both work hard, for too long, for little pay with no guarantee that it will work out….the one with entrepreneurial spirit works for the love of working, for the love of learning, and for the desire to leave a legacy.

The worker often states: "I just want to make enough to pay my bills." The worker operates in survival mode. The worker fears change, embraces the status quo, clocks his or her time, and works toward retirement.

Entrepreneurs are just really finding their ZOOM, their stride, as they approach retirement age. The idea of retirement doesn't really speak to the entrepreneur.

The worker views life as a line, the journey from point A to point B.

A _____B

The entrepreneur views life as a circle – not in terms of a beginning or an end, but as a continuous steady stream of free-flowing interconnected events.

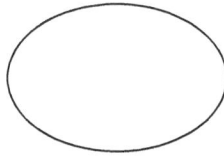

We all know when we feel passion, for it is relentless in pushing us on. The entrepreneurial spirit doesn't stop because it reaches a certain age, or because of a failed idea, or lack of funding, or any other external reason. Understand it is viewed by the possessor as a good thing, a treasured part of us. We keep setting one block on top of another. Oh sure, we occasionally have to rearrange them, but that's okay because we know that's part of the deal.

The entrepreneurial spirit is an intrinsic passion to create something that changes the world.

We are going to introduce Carl at this point. We will take very good look at Carl as we go along in our journey. Now Carl is a very passionate person. He'll work hard, he will teach you, and he micromanages you, even though he himself is not a disciplined person. What he is, though, is a thinker and a starter. Does any of this sound familiar? Carl can't figure out *how to get out of his own way*. Carl is stuck.

If we actually assigned others to manage some of these tasks Carl has assumed and consider these opportunities for our workers to coach and mentor others towards their success, we would keep the ball rolling in the right direction.

What are you passionate about? Consider this: What is getting in your way? What is keeping you from achieving your goals, your desires, and your success? What is one thing you can begin to do differently today?

3. FOCUS

verb \ ˈfōkəs \

: (of a person or their eyes) adapt to the prevailing level of light and become able to see clearly.

: pay particular attention to.

"You can do anything as long as you have the passion, the drive, the focus, and the support." Sabrina Bryan

This whole thought is very amusing for a business owner who fights this battle every waking minute, yet it is a battle worth fighting. You know that being driven by a passion while maintaining focus allows for great success.

What makes one entrepreneur successful, and what keeps one entrepreneur stuck?

Both are hardworking and passionate about their ideas. Both possess the resilience and energy to do whatever it takes for a successful start-up. The difference often comes down to focus, balance, and self-discipline.

Intrinsic passion fuels the ZOOM of the entrepreneur, but if passion is not managed, it can produce a blurred lens or an inability to focus your attention. The entrepreneur is attracted to "start-ups" and can move quickly from start-up to start-up, never really seeing one idea or project through to fruition. This produces that adrenaline rush on which many entrepreneurs feed. This lack of focus can be very costly in terms of time, energy, and financing.

The entrepreneurial head is often full of goals and ideas. However, we struggle to slow down and really define those goals. We all have things we want to achieve in our lives: getting into better shape, building a successful business, raising a wonderful family, writing a best-selling book, winning a championship, and so on.

The successful entrepreneur understands goals are good short-term motivators, but without a clear, organized, established system, those goals often aren't accomplished. Take, for instance, writing a book. Your goal might be to complete a published book in one year. Many will start that book, work on it for a couple of weeks, and then talk about writing a book for the remainder of the year. At the end of the year, the book is not written, and the goal is either dismissed or extended. We tell ourselves we just didn't have time. Truth is we do have the time -- we just don't commit to a system. A book writing system might be defined as building in a specific time for writing, for example, writing twenty minutes every day. A system is where the rubber meets the road; it's walking your talk. A goal is focused on the end result. The system is focused on the specific activities, the "doing" that produces the end result.

On the other hand, being passionate without maintaining focus will keep you in the rocking chair (a lot of action with no results).

We have to maintain clarity of purpose and not let the steps in the process become the end game. As important as they are; they are just steps. Distraction, distraction, distraction, it's going to happen, but we need to learn how to manage it and not let it destroy perspective, because it will.

Focus is about putting your mind and energy toward the right things at the right time. To do this you would first need to raise your awareness of what breaks your focus or what distractions are in your way. Once you understand what your specific distraction triggers are, then you have everything you need to address those distractions and commit to changing your behavior.

Focus is also about knowing when our energy level is at its highest point during the day, and then planning to tackle our hardest tasks when we are the strongest. We want to know when we are the strongest and then act.

Focus is about taking care of ourselves along the way -- getting enough sleep, eating right, exercising the stress away. If all our energy is spent dealing with these fundamentals of life, then it stands to reason that other important things are not getting accomplished. Time marches on, we find ourselves at the end of another year, and our goals haven't been met. Flight attendants encourage passengers to fix the oxygen mask to themselves first and then help others. That speaks directly to us about self-care -- managing from strength.

Focus is about seeing our path, preparing to run the race, planning our strategies, focusing our ZOOM, and consistently putting one foot in front of the other until we achieve the success we desire.

If we were going to run a marathon, most people would not be able just to put on their running shoes, show up to the race, and succeed at finishing the whole 26.2 miles. A marathon, like a business, takes careful discipline, planning, and training. We might have the best idea and the finances to fund the idea, but without a focused, disciplined plan, chances are slim that our business will succeed.

Many times the very thing that entrepreneurs struggle with is just slowing down, thinking about what needs to be done, writing down or communicating a specific plan, and then gathering the resources to execute the plan. The approach of an unfocused manager looks more like having a great idea and jumping into the deep end before learning to swim.

Impulsivity (omit that) needs to be focused or managed. It's a challenge to control the adrenaline rush that comes with the "start-up" of a business idea. However, the lack of focus or systems can get us in trouble or delay our success.

Systems require self-discipline. Systems require resilience and focus. The entrepreneur who thrives on the "start-up" adrenaline often avoids systems. Once something feels structured and repetitive, the entrepreneur often gets bored and begins looking for the next "shiny" thing. Your idea simply cannot ZOOM forward without a clear, focused business plan!

Carl: OK, where is our friend Carl when it comes to focus? Once again, all the great ideas are there, but you see Carl can't manage systems that are already in place. He just wants to keep moving, and while he believes systems are probably a good idea, he just can't slow down long enough to create and employ them. He just can't.

Carl desperately needs to employ a doer who will be passionate and focused on systems to accomplish Carl's vision for the company. So Carl continues to come and go in his business, sometimes micromanaging and other times checking out. This creates confusion for all employees, and the company's progress gets stalled.

Carl is frustrated. He can't seem to understand why his goals are not being met. He works hard, he puts in long days, but he is spinning his wheels and not getting any traction for the future. Once again, avoidance rears its ugly head.

4. SELF-DISCIPLINE

noun \ self ˈdisəplən \

: the ability to control one's feelings and overcome one's weaknesses.

: the ability to pursue what one thinks is right despite temptations to abandon it.

"Self-discipline is an act of cultivation. It requires you to connect today's action to tomorrow's results. There's a season for sowing and a season for reaping. Self-discipline helps you know which is which." Gary Ryan Blair

Self-discipline is the correction or regulation of oneself for the sake of improvement. For many entrepreneurs, their strength is not found in developing and working a system. The entrepreneur typically excels at the vision, the idea, and the start-up. The entrepreneur does not necessarily need to be the one working all the parts and nuances of the system.

Frankly, the entrepreneur achieves success by understanding his or her own strengths and weaknesses and then acquiring or hiring a team to define and work the system to achieve success.

An entrepreneur can actually throw off the equilibrium of the team by constantly verbalizing idea after idea of the next shiny thing. The successful entrepreneur has the ability to focus the lens for the "wide angle, ZOOM out view" of the project, but also the "ZOOM in, system focus" of the project.

Consider this analogy. If you drive your car focusing only on the big picture, say three stoplights ahead, it is likely you will run into the car right in front of you. If you have a destination (goal) in mind, but you just drive erratically without a plan, without knowledge of the roads to take, it is logical that you might not get there, or you will expend unnecessary time, fuel, and energy getting to that destination.

Ever heard yourself say: "I don't really have a plan. I'm just too busy trying to get through the day to have a plan. My people can't stay on any course. I can't take the time. Are you kidding me, a plan? I wouldn't know where to begin."

Does any of this sound familiar? Well, if it does, just understand that until you do have a plan, nothing will ever change. All great accomplishments are the result of having a plan. Just imagine a great general going into battle without a plan. Without a plan, we often spend much more time maintaining the status quo than it would take to create a plan, obtain employee buy-in, and actually move forward.

It all begins with order and input from others. This can be accomplished by using the strategic planning process. It's important to understand and use this process as we begin to get organized through planning.

Many dollars can be saved and many more generated by this process. This only enhances everyone's well-being and puts a positive motion in place for your business and, guess what; your job gets easier and much more rewarding. To do this, get information on strategic planning. It's readily available -- use it. Make the commitment. This can be the beginning of positive movement in a company. Commit, do it, and be consistent. You'll be glad you did.

Very few small companies or even larger companies go through the process I've described above and, therefore, the cycle of literally going around the same circle over and over again is never broken.

We have to find a way to establish direction that depends on systems and goals and not just your dreams. If not, you'll just wear out as the company fails to thrive, and your good employees will leave you in search of greener pastures.

So, to make the step toward progress and freedom, we have to figure out why we haven't progressed and then move on. If you have a strategic plan in place, you have a way to measure your progression toward your goals, financial and otherwise. We have to understand not only that we're stuck, but why we're stuck. Oh my, we have to change. This sounds like work. We only have to do it once. We're already working very hard, but isn't that the point? We are working way too hard.

Discipline plays a huge role in focus and eventual accomplishment. We know that anything we have ever been really successful at required discipline, and wow, we had it when we accomplished that success. We have seen people with advanced college degrees who couldn't focus long enough to grow or systematize their businesses. This is extremely frustrating, and I continue to wonder: Why?

The reason many of us lack self-discipline is the failure to acknowledge our weaknesses. Whether that is a doughnut that is a downfall to your diet, trying to quit smoking, or whatever you deceive yourself about, too often people try to pretend their weaknesses don't exist or minimize them to the point of inaction.

It's a Superhero complex: We simply think we can do it all and be it all. This is especially true for small businesses where in the beginning the entrepreneurs wore all the hats. They were the worker, accountant, marketer, etc. Pride gets in the way. We were the king/queen of the business.

When the business grows and takes over every waking moment of our lives, we take pride in our self-discipline to get the job done. Once we start hiring employees, we struggle to delegate responsibility – really to trust that our employees will do it as well as we did. We continue to hold on too tight, and burnout sets in. That is when all our bad habits begin to get in the way of our self-discipline.

We tell ourselves, we have worked hard; we deserve to take the day off. We begin inconsistently leading our business. This becomes our new work pattern, and our goals simply aren't being consistently worked on, and therefore, not consistently met. You put your employees on a rollercoaster ride that they never get off of and eventually you wear them out.

Example: Carl just couldn't get quality of product from his employees. His customers were unhappy, and he spent more time putting out fires than actually creating new business. This wasn't what he had in mind when he created his business.

He still has a ton of energy, but this fire-fighting is wearing him out. You see, he just couldn't find or keep good people. It was just so frustrating.

Carl became convinced that if he wanted everything done right, then he would have to do it himself.

Carl was working "in" his business, not on his business. Carl was exhausted, his personal life was suffering, and he was even starting to question why he was continuing the enterprise.

Carl's business was declining, but it didn't have to decline. Carl just needed to recognize his own strengths and weaknesses, and get out of his own way!

Just like Carl, we have to establish a clear plan to get "real" with self-discipline. Often the entrepreneurial type struggles to make the plan and stick with the plan. Our personalities typically don't like routine. The routine is the very thing we need to put the right plan in place, and to assure that we consistently work that plan through to completion.

Routine makes entrepreneurs emotionally uncomfortable. It's normal to want to avoid pain and discomfort. But in the business world, if you avoid pain and discomfort long enough, there will be consequences. Instead, practice allowing yourself to experience uncomfortable emotions like frustration and boredom. Fight the emotions that produce impulsivity, and you will increase your self-discipline.

No pain no gain, as they say. Self-discipline is the hard part of success.

Truly you have the energy to do whatever you put your mind to, which is evident in the success you have already achieved.

What we are talking about here is accepting that self-discipline needs to be shored up to achieve your next level of success. Just as a book will not write itself, your business can and will stagnate without passion, focus, and self-discipline.

Start today by truly looking at your strengths and weaknesses and then making a plan to overcome your challenges.

You might need a mentor to help clarify this for you. Sometimes it is difficult to be honest with ourselves. We get caught in the mental whirlpool of applying the same thoughts we have always had and getting the same results we have always gotten.

Asking others to evaluate our leadership skills and our business can provide a clearer perspective of our business. If we listen without defense, we just might get out of our own way and ZOOM toward success.

"Everybody starts at the top, and then has the problem of staying there. Lasting accomplishment, however, is still

achieved through a long, slow climb and self-discipline." Helen Hayes

If you were weak and unable to climb a ladder, you might consider being self-disciplined enough to strengthen your body through exercise so you could climb the next rung.

Ask yourself: What are you currently justifying that is holding you back?

Once you have identified what is holding you back, make a plan and begin taking different actions, today! If you can't see it, ask others to help you identify it for you. Recycling the same thoughts produces the same results. Break that cycle, get a coach or mentor to show you a different way.

After all, self-discipline is the key to reaching your goals and creating a better life. Get out of your own way with this one step, and experience the sheer joy of ZOOMing forward toward your success!

5. ACCOUNTABILITY

noun \ əˌkoun(t)əˈbilədē\

: an obligation or willingness to accept responsibility or to account for one's actions.

"Accountability breeds response-ability." Stephen Covey

Accountability will help us be disciplined. To whom are we accountable? Who can help us ZOOM? Are we getting too close to our EGO here? Maybe, huh. Well, get over yourself and lead the way. It seems that when we don't want to be accountable, our attitude has a strong tendency to broadcast this message to the troops: "Hey, do as I say, not as I do."

Building systems takes discipline, and discipline requires accountability. Good systems are key to profitable growth and the retention of good people. So build some systems, and establish your accountability.

Accountability is kind of like getting motivated. Author and motivational speaker, Zig Ziglar, used to say, "People often say that motivation doesn't last. Well, neither does bathing -- that's why we recommend it daily." Find your accountability, get motivated, and be consistent, and the discipline will be there.

The key to accountability is having a strong "why"! If you are not clear on what you want and why you want it, you simply will not feel the passion, focus, self-discipline, and accountability for that goal. You will waste time. Having a clear "why" is the stuff that gets you out of bed in the morning. It is what gets you focused! Ask yourself on a regular basis: Is what I'm doing right now moving me toward or away from my goals? What can I do right now that will ZOOM my "why"?

Promise yourself that you won't waste time on things that get in the way of your "why." Be accountable to yourself.

We will certainly agree with those who say this is hard, because it is; all the good stuff is hard. The tough get going.

They say it's lonely at the top, and perhaps that's true because we set ourselves and our businesses up that way. If you struggle with self-discipline, then you will struggle with accountability.

If we are accountable only to ourselves, then it's easy to justify to yourself the why's or why not's of how you do things. It's easy to put things off, or give excuses for doing things the way you have always done them, even though those things have seen their day and are impeding success.

Ask yourself why hiring a consultant often works; it's because it builds in accountability for change in you and in your business. Consultants often can see from a fresh perspective the roadblocks that are holding you back in your business.

They can point out the entrenched grooves you have forged in your path, those times when you say, "Well, that's how we have always done it." Some of those things worked when it was you and one other who started the business, but don't really apply any more.

Some of those things produce "fear of the unknown." The old saying that you can't see the forest for the trees really applies here. When you are blinded by all the small details, it is impossible to see the big picture anymore. The incremental changes you make aren't big enough to produce the change necessary to propel your success.

Accountability partners can be found in many places. Perhaps it's a consultant, a business or life coach, a professional counselor, another successful professional, a mentor at a business incubator, Volunteer Lawyers and Accountants for the Arts, or all of the above. It has to be someone outside of your company and – most important -- outside of your own head. This is someone who doesn't have an emotional connection to you and your company's current method of operation. Those are the people who will be able to communicate a fresh perspective and challenge you to make the changes necessary to find your ZOOM.

Why do many of us avoid hiring a consultant or even talking to another professional about our businesses? We hesitate because of fear, because it makes us vulnerable, because of the transparency, or maybe we're afraid we'll be judged.

Perhaps it's just pride; we think we know it all. Or perhaps it is our fear of trusting others, or just wanting to take credit for all the decisions that are made. However you define the fear, if you want true change to take place, you have to get real with what is going on and be accountable to make the necessary, sometimes hard changes to ZOOM your business forward.

Nothing so effectually robs the mind of all of its power of acting and reasoning as does fear.

Carl: If one desires a simpler life, then we design systems that incorporate accountability into our operation. When "something" happened when Carl left town for a week to attend a funeral, Carl couldn't or wouldn't incorporate answerability and wouldn't seek help in designing systems that would have allowed for smoother sailing in his absence. The rest is history. Oh, Carl!

So to put a little finer point on this concept, please know that accountability is the key to every successful venture -- business, sports team, and, yes, individual success. It sharpens focus, and this sharpened focus is the end goal. Focused passion, self-discipline, and accountability produce productivity and positive change.

Accountability through systems that are SUPPORTED by everyone involved will produce outstanding results. Be committed, don't stop, come on, stay with it, find the energy, it can be done, and it is done every day. Find your ZOOM, get with it, no excuses! This will impact your and everyone else's future. Start right now, put the book down, and make a commitment. Write it down, and let's ZOOM!

6. **FEAR**

noun \ ˈfir

: an unpleasant emotion caused by the belief that someone or something is dangerous, likely to cause pain, or a threat.

verb \ ˈfir

: be afraid of (someone or something) as likely to be dangerous, painful, or threatening.

"Fear stifles our thinking and our actions. It creates indecisiveness that results in stagnation. I have known talented people who procrastinate indefinitely rather than risk failure. Lost opportunities cause erosion of confidence, and the downward spiral begins." Charles Stanley

There will be consequences for whatever we do, whether we act or don't. Generally speaking, the consequences of inaction are the ones that destroy momentum (ZOOM), energy, and possibility.

The consequences of action may be failure, success, a learning experience, and the realization that we are alive and going forward. Know the benefits of failure, and let go of your fear. The mistakes we make will teach us great lessons and build real strength. Come on, go for it!

Where does the fear come from? Why are we afraid when others aren't? What if we did something and it didn't work? If we don't experience this once in a while, we're just not taking enough risks. Try it! Failing won't be as earth-shaking as you think. There's that EGO again. I am not advocating foolish decision-making or seat-of-the-pants management, but rather calculated risk-taking, which will give you a good batting average (but you can't expect a thousand).

To push through the fear, first you have to recognize that you are stuck. Once you clearly see fear is holding you back, the next step is recognizing your level of discontentment with the ways things are. Although most people skip or ignore their discontentment, it is the discontentment that produces the desire to change. Why would any of us do the hard work to change a bad habit, if that habit wasn't producing unease in our lives?

Take time to sit in your discontentment. Picture a big pile of garbage, and picture yourself in the middle of it. You could put some perfume on it and ignore that it's there, but that will only work for so long, right? The problem is still there. The only real path is to admit it is there, clean it up, and make a plan for change, so it doesn't pile up over and over again.

Once you recognize your displeasure, the next stage is awareness -- getting honest with yourself, asking and listening to others, really getting a grasp on what is happening or not happening that is producing fear and keeping you stalled on your path.

Sometimes this is the point when a consultant or non-biased person can help you really see your patterns, really assess your business. This is not a quick pass at the one, small, safe part of your business, but really opening yourself up to a deep analysis. It requires you to have an open mind and to be willing to get feedback on the good, the bad, and the ugly.

Armed with this information, you can now move to the action stage, the ZOOM of change. This is the stage where you have to trust yourself and others, push through the fear of change or the unknown, and start blazing a different path.

This is the point where a plan needs to be put in place, communication at all levels within the organization needs to be systematically handled, and defined action needs to begin and be sustained until progress is recognized.

Many entrepreneurs start these action plans and get bored with the process, and so the plans become just the "latest, greatest" thing. This behavior trains your people just to wait you out until the next "change" comes along. As entrepreneurs, we have to fight our desire to get that adrenaline rush of the next shiny thing.

What we are talking about here is an intentional understanding of what needs to change, what it takes to produce the change, and tracking the outcome of the change. It is recognizing the momentum for the business and riding that train to success. It is creating your ZOOM, through focused leadership. You have to recognize the fear, and then do it anyway. Fear is crumbled one step at a time. Pushing through is often the only way to address what produces anxiety in ourselves. Ask yourself: What is the worst thing that can happen if I change? Then ask yourself: What is the worst thing that can happen if I don't change? Then pick one, and implement your plan.

Most people react from a fear base when they feel out of control. The lack of control produces behavior that is on the ends – either avoidance or micromanaging. Both avoidance and micromanaging create a difficult working relationship.

Your great employees will be upset when you are avoiding them or avoiding making a decision; and those same employees will not deal well with being micromanaged. Take a moment to assess what feels out of control, or what you are projecting "might" happen in the situation. Gather your team, and engage them in finding a solution. Often you will be surprised at what they come up with for a solution. The goal is not 100 percent trust, because that does not exist. The goal is to move forward, even if that means a couple of steps backward first.

Fear and guilt are so closely aligned; they can even become allies, one supporting the other. As a good or even great leader, we need to spend a certain amount of time identifying and then removing the obstacles to our and, therefore, our team's success.

This is an obligation, not an option, if we are really trying to be fair. Understand that if you are not seen as fair, you will lose all of your good and great people. Find and keep employees who are committed to outstanding, productive actions. Keeping employees on your team who are weighing you down won't cut it. If you were trying to row a boat and half of the oarsmen weren't rowing, how long do you think your good, strong rowers will be motivated to move things forward? You will wear them out both mentally and physically.

We have heard of holding onto an employee long past the time they should be working for you, because of fear of not finding a replacement. Meanwhile, that same employee is throwing you and the company under the bus at every opportunity. Some false sense of loyalty is at play. You are loyal to them as a long-term employee, but are they loyal to you?

Sometimes the kindest thing you can do for someone is to let him or her go. I wonder how many people have had their lives turned around by being fired. Pain produces change. People who are settled down into their comfort zone get complacent.

Complacency doesn't produce ZOOM for your business. Don't settle for second best; hire and maintain a motivated team!

Carl: You would think from a distance that this man had no fear, but I assure you it was there. His jovial fun-loving nature covered up his underlying truth. Carl lived in fear. Carl was threatened or fearful of talented employees. He unconsciously was fearful they knew more than he did. He felt vulnerable in the areas of self-discipline and leadership.

He overcompensated by alternately avoiding or micromanaging his employees. He identified with being a "nice" guy and created an environment in which the weaker employees took advantage of him, and the strong employees were frustrated with the entire system.

The inconsistency produced fear in all of his employees, and that fear produced turnover. Carl was worn out trying to hire and maintain good employees. Carl would often say: "I'd have a great business if it weren't for the people I have to manage."

If Carl had only taken action to correct the fear-causing centers of his business, he would recognize employees who are just "along for the ride" and would take action to replace them with employees who are engaged in the process of propelling the boat forward with energy and passion. His energy would be redirected in finding employees who embody the very attributes of ZOOM!

7. LEADERSHIP

noun \ ˈlēdərˌSHip\

: the action of leading a group of people or an organization.

: the state or position of being a leader.

"A leader is one who knows the way, goes the way, and shows the way." John C. Maxwell

Paying lip service to caring is not caring. Remember deeds, not words, are the proof of caring, and nobody in your company cares until they know that you care.

Leaders are courageous. Are you courageous? Courage has been defined as action in the face of fear. It seems right. That is a characteristic of a great leader. What else will be expected of you? Well, you'll need to be seen as fair, and this has to be how employees see you, not only how you see yourself.

All great organizations have really strong leadership. It doesn't always have to be the owner, but somebody has to be the leader. The organization won't grow successfully without great leadership. The decision is yours. Be the leader here, and make the decision to be in charge.

Okay, what stops us from being in charge? We mean, really in charge. We often see owners of smaller companies fail to make decisions and lack the ability to trust anyone else to make those decisions. So the decisions were not made; it just didn't happen. Why?

Sometimes the indecision is based on history. Maybe you have been burned by an employee in the past. Maybe you started the business and were in charge of everything all the time, so now you're struggling to relinquish control. It is true that no one will do a particular thing exactly like you, but it also is true that there may be many ways to accomplish the same result. It's not logical to expect to grow your businesses, if you continue to try and do all and be all in that business.

Carl: You know Carl is bigger than life, but that doesn't make him a good leader. It just means you can't miss him. Often with Carl there is no separation from the troops. Sometimes he just wants to be one of the boys, but it's very hard to lead without separation. Sometimes he discusses his often precarious financial situation with the troops.

You should lead from a slight distance and from strength. The troops are looking for these qualities.

Let's test this theory by establishing a leadership group in your organization. You will help not only in the development of others, but also spread the burden of planning and decision-making over at least three people. Now you have to have faith in these folks, so choose them carefully. Empower them at some level of decision-making, and trust them.

Remember that coaching and trusting go hand in hand in their development. DO NOT SMOTHER THEM! Be sure to hold them accountable in some systematic way.

Within this leadership group, there needs to be constant leadership development. There are many opportunities through study, meetings with leadership development professionals, and local leadership classes. Avail yourself of these opportunities, and take this development step. Set the standard for anyone who aspires to be part of your leadership group.

Leadership should continue training as well. It just stands to reason that the best leaders are the ones who will build the strongest organizations, and strong organizations benefit everyone in them.

Remember to establish an edge over your competition in every area possible, and leadership development is definitely one of those areas that will pay substantial dividends.

Start today. Don't wait. It's too important; always do the important first. As the man says, "It doesn't cost; it pays." So start right now. Don't wait, because the energy will fade. Do it

now! ZOOM!

8. HARDWIRED

adjective \ ˌhärdˈwī(ə)rd

: behavior that is hardwired as by genetics and the way the brain is made, rather than learned by experience.

"I feel that as long as you are honest, you have the opportunity to grow. It's when you shut down, go into denial, and try to start hiding things from yourself and others, that's when you lock in certain behaviors and attitudes that keep you stuck."
Tracy McMillan

It's just the way I am. I'm hardwired, folks. Do you really think you're hardwired to be exactly who you presently are? Isn't this a little like saying you're not in charge of you or that you haven't been shaped by experience? Please always know that you, and your thinking controls who you are. Your thinking is who you are, and the minute you change your thinking, you change who you are, that very minute. Thank you, Dennis Deaton. The author of "The Book on Mind Management," a book we strongly recommend for everyone. When someone makes a comment like "That's just the way I am," they are really saying, "This isn't working, and I don't know how to do it differently." This is another example of fear-based behavior and another opportunity to get a mentor who will be honest with you and help you walk a different path. Don't be a person who has given up hope that things can be different. You have to be willing to get the door opened up again to a new thought and new action, and be willing to learn a new way. Knowing that you have the ability to change your thinking on the spot should start your engine. If it doesn't, you're just not ready yet. We are going to assume that since you bought this book, you're probably at least thinking about a different approach to life and your career. OK, now take a minute, and grab onto that thought real tight. We'll wait.

Motivational speaker Jim Rohn famously said that we are the average of the five people with whom we spend the most time. Let's take a peek at that concept or who those five people might be. Certainly our parents would have been there early on, and maybe a teacher, a coach, and certainly those first friends with whom we associated, and certainly our siblings.

Who are those five people today? Take another minute, and examine their traits -- intelligence (surround yourself with people who are smarter than you and see what happens), attitude, drive, and values. Those might be a few of the things we'd consider, and then examine your own traits, and you might want to turn the light up a little. Just remember the very minute you change your thinking, your life changes. We are not saying this is easy, but then none of the good stuff is easy. CHANGE YOUR THINKING, AND CHANGE YOUR LIFE.

Please know that all we have brought up here is absolutely true, and the benefits are huge. Plan to read Dennis Deaton's first book, "The Book on Mind Management", and then go from there.

What is hardwired are your strengths. Embrace those strengths, and continue to build on them. Continue to learn and grow. Self-help author and motivational speaker Anthony Robbins said, "If you're not growing, you're dying." Being a lifelong learner is a lifestyle, not an event. We must always be motivated to learn.

How many older people do you know who have failed to learn technology and, as a result, have become dinosaurs in the business world? They often say, "I'll just continue to do this manually, the way I always have." The project takes them twice as long, and is less fluid for the team. How many examples can we think of where invention has improved our lives, substantially? What if those inventors said, "That's just the way I am. I'm hardwired that way"?

Your unique talents will leave the world a better place, if you decide to share them. Holing up in a safe place, stuck in some negative identity, does nothing for you, your company, or your world.

So are you growing, or are you dying? Or are you just

procrastinating about that decision?

9. PROCRASTINATION

Noun\ prə ̩krastəˈnāSH(ə)n

: the action of delaying or postponing something.

"Procrastination is the bad habit of putting off until the day after tomorrow what should have been done the day before yesterday." Napoleon Hill

Consider this inner dialogue: We are either lazy or afraid. We are not sure which. We want to just think about it later. Maybe it's change we are afraid of. Suppose for a minute that we decided to embrace change; after all, it is the future. What would that look like, and what would happen if we did? OK, that all sounds like a lot of work! So we get lazy!

When we finish taking a good look inside, understand that what we are putting off is sabotaging our businesses. Then we have a decision to make -- and we know this is hard -- but we need to put our big boy or big girl pants on, and make this decision NOW.

There are three ways this can go: 1) stay the way we are, 2) change, or 3) if we are not the leader, hire one. What's the advice? "Lead, follow, or get out of the way." And it is the truth.

What happens when the procrastination goes away and a "Sense of Urgency" arrives? Now enters energy, a key ingredient of success. The good and great employees, if you have some left, really come to life. The poor or actively disconnected employees will leave, and we would prefer that be sooner than later. Perhaps we can facilitate that. Someone has taken charge of human resources. Now progress can really be made.

Procrastinators are negative, if not partially defeated folks, and these tendencies are in and of themselves self-defeating. Changing this about ourselves is a major undertaking, and we can't do it alone. You're going to need a coach, someone to hold you accountable.

Procrastination can be a by-product of perfectionism. You might wonder, what's the problem with wanting something to be perfect? You might hear yourself saying things like, "Something worth doing is worth doing right." Certainly no one wants to dispute the benefit of doing quality work; perfectionism, however, can lead to the paralysis called procrastination. Wanting something perfect will often cause people not to start at all.

Procrastination is guilt's ugly step-sister -- when we know we should be getting something accomplished and we keep putting it off; once again we are living with guilt. We have to stop "should-ing" on ourselves.

A place to start dealing with your procrastination is to listen for the word "should" in your internal dialogue. Any time you are stating "I should have," or even "I shouldn't have," stop for a moment, look at what the issue is, and think about why you are avoiding the project.

Once you have awareness of what "should" happen, go about making a plan to get it accomplished. Fight the urge for perfectionism. We have stated how important accountability is to any sort of personal growth and/or change. So find a coach, and become accountable. This will involve a change in our thinking, and the minute our thinking changes, our actions will follow.

If you don't feel you can actually change that much, past performance over a long period of time is usually a good indicator. You decide! If you feel you can't accomplish a necessary task, then find someone who can and stay out of the way.

Think about someone else who can support the project or take the project and run with it. Just get out of limbo. Consider tackling part of the project; so at a minimum, you are at least moving it forward. Get started; don't wallow there in your paralysis. Start walking toward that goal. Don't waste one more minute of your ZOOM. The benefits to your company as a result of great LEADERSHIP and ACTION will be amazing.

10. ANONYMOUS

Noun\ aNGˈzīədē

: a feeling of worry, nervousness, or unease, typically about an imminent event or something with an uncertain outcome.

: desire to do something, typically accompanied by unease.

"Even though you may want to move forward in your life, you may have one foot on the brakes. In order to be free we must learn how to let go. Release the hurt. Release the fear. Refuse to entertain your old pain. The energy it takes to hang onto the past is holding us back from a new life. What is it we need to let go of today?" Mary Mannin Morrissey

Let's see, when are we at our best? Is it when we are tense, when we are anxious, angry, or perhaps when we are frustrated, disappointed, or when we are hyped? We are at our best when we are relaxed and focused. Sure, everyone experiences aforementioned feelings. We urge you to get past them as quickly as possible. We simply cannot progress to a better place unless we do. If we can adopt a real sense of enjoyment in taking on the challenges of life rather than dreading them, it will change our lives significantly.

Sports can be very intense, especially at the professional level. There are careers and livelihoods at stake here. Trainers teach all those who participate in sports to have an athletic stance. It allows one to anticipate rather than just react both mentally and physically. In both golf and baseball, we are taught to hold the club or bat in a gentle fashion. A firm grip will tighten the arm muscles and slow down the swing resulting in a shorter shot.

If we can relax in our approach to what we do and how we address others, we will have the potential for great success. If not, we can predict failure, and the lack of desired results will only increase the frustration.

"We have to know we can and we will. If we've never done it, how can we know this? We can know this only when we've done it." Steven Pressfield.

It seems that everything we do to be successful requires courage, action in the face of fear. Our desire for success has to be stronger than our fear. The fear seems to diminish only when we've conquered it. This, my friends, is worth experiencing. It puts us in a whole different place. It's also a place we have to get to if we are to experience the real success we are looking for in all that we do.

Worry is a waste of time, so stop it. Being tense is the result of being worried and not only causes us to grip the bat too hard, which results in failure, but also causes our bodies to respond with poor health. It causes positive people to flee. Worry, tenseness, fear of failure, procrastination, all of it results in our approaching our business effort ill-prepared for success.

If you have ever operated a piece of equipment with a slow-running battery, you know how frustrating getting the job done with it can be. It is critical that you manage your energy by focusing it on activities that produce the results you desire. Wasting your internal resources on guilt, procrastination, and fear will produce a rollercoaster, white- knuckle ride for you, your employees, and your business. It creates confusion, it stalls decisions, and it all becomes one giant unproductive cycle producing exhaustion. It's like running a race where someone keeps moving the finish line when you get close. Your employees will give up and just clock their time with this kind of leadership.

Think about being taken to an amusement park and put on a rollercoaster ride for two days straight. How do you think you would be feeling after those two days? You might have felt pretty good with the adrenaline rush of the start, but after sustaining the ups and downs of that ride for two straight days, you might not have that same good feeling. Think about what your employees are experiencing, if you are creating this type of environment in your business.

Self-care in terms of relaxation is critical to your success. Exhaustion has many consequences. Take a step back to observe your behavior as if you are watching your own movie. What advice would you give yourself? If your friend or colleague was experiencing the same issues as you are, what would you tell him to do or not do? Often we have great clarity when it comes to other people, but have blinders on with our own lives and businesses. That is why having an accountability partner is critical. That person can see the ride you are on and help you stop your negative cycles.

What we are asking is just RELAX, but be aware. We can't abandon planning or a strategic and tactical approach.

Example: Carl had, with the assistance of a consultant, established a list of changes he had to make, and they both agreed this would make a major difference in Carl's business.

Carl paid the consultant faithfully for three years. Even so, Carl acted on only 10 percent of the recommended changes -- the easy ones.

Carl was procrastinating. He held everything inside; yet on the outside, he appeared relaxed and pleasant. Carl was building an internal bomb. Carl would let the frustration build and then lash out and start the process all over again. This passive/aggressive behavior was like riding that rollercoaster ride over and over for his employees. He wasn't volatile; he would let the frustration build for a year or two before lashing out. His employees were tiring of trying to figure out what Carl wanted done in the business. Carl's lack of courage and action produced exhaustion for himself and his employees, which in turn, produced a sluggish business. Making the shift to put his energy into planning, executing, and communicating a clear target for the business will get everyone rowing the boat in the same direction, as a team, with focused energy toward the destination.

Isn't it time to relax, regroup, and release whatever is holding you back from accomplishing your goals?

11. GUILT

Noun\ gilt

: the fact of having committed a specified or implied offense or crime.

"Negative emotions like loneliness, envy, and guilt have an important role to play in a happy life; they're big, flashing signs that something needs to change." Gretchen Rubin

Dictionaries define guilt as a feeling of responsibility or remorse for some offense, crime, or wrongdoing, whether real or imagined have seen so many people not make changes in their businesses when they know they have the wrong person in a certain position or just have an individual in their company who is actually doing harm to the organization. We used to think that the owner just wasn't strong enough to make the change. We now think while that certainly happens in some cases, the prevailing reason it is done or not done is out of a sense of guilt.

We want to suggest to those who are not acting to improve their organization by eliminating a roadblock individual that if they want to have some truly justifiable sense of guilt, just consider all the harm being done to your organization. Our companies support employees and their families, and our failure to fire a poor performer causes frustration among good and even great employees.

You know, chances are you are not doing the roadblock employee any favors either. In fact, you are just reinforcing and rewarding poor or bad behavior by not addressing the situation in a manner that will resolve the problem.

So let's examine the harm. Unhappy employees really do affect our customers, especially the demanding customer. Understand please that they do not hesitate to inform our customers and fellow employees of what a terrible organization we have. That's the only way they can justify their own behavior. These employees are the actively disengaged employees, the very ones who want to see you fail because their unhealthy attitudes can only be justified by your failure. Sure, they'll go down with you, but this fact is not dealt with, because then the soap opera would end -- and that does not serve their purpose. Let's address unhappy people here. The only person we can make happy for the long term is us. We can inspire and lead others, we can develop others and create opportunities, but happiness comes from within, not from without. No one can be responsible for someone else's happiness. Each person has choices. Each person makes decisions regarding his or her own happiness.

The very real harm that is done here is the result of maintaining an unhealthy status quo. This is the exact opposite of leadership and is seen by everybody else as weakness. The weak have been and always will be taken advantage of. Prosperity does not spring from this well.

The good or potentially good employees will only be discouraged by this situation, although many will profess that it's going to be OK. Once they can no longer carry the burden, they either capitulate, continue to suffer the consequences, or quit. Now we are justified in feeling guilty about that. Ah, success.

Guilt can be habit-forming. Most people don't know how to process guilt feelings. Many people take responsibility or feel guilty about things squarely out of their control.

Carl on guilt: This is not a problem for Carl. He is not burdened by the weight of guilt. He would just ignore it and get on with the business of going forward.

Many of those with whom we have worked have their greatest difficulty with dismissing a problem employee so they can avoid the accompanying guilt. These people are usually longer term employees who are well entrenched, but totally disconnected when it comes to the team's effort and/or success. Someone has to take the part of holding others accountable. This type of employee is cancerous for an organization. A leader holds people accountable. A leader does not just take on all the problems of the team, stress about it, and assume guilt when situations set the company back.

A leader provides the ZOOM for the team to assess the situation, develop the solution, and put the plan in place to move the company forward. Guilt will have us in the corner feeling sorry for ourselves.

ZOOM will represent the energy of leading the team to victory.

12. COMPETITION

Noun\ ˌkämpəˈtiSH(ə)n

: the person or people with whom one is competing, especially in a commercial or sporting arena; the opposition.

"The healthiest competition occurs when average people win by putting in above-average effort." Colin Powell

Competition is perceived in vastly different ways by people in general, and we guess that applies to those of us in business as well. We have seen those who relish the idea of being in a competitive situation in business and those to whom the thought of having to compete upsets them. In other words, if we don't enjoy a monopoly on producing goods or providing a service, we feel threatened.

When we were still very young in business, we felt threatened by a new competitor who had the resources to do a great deal of media advertising. When we voiced concern about this new competitor to our boss, he simply stated that they were only heightening the awareness of the service we all provided. It seems, from that moment on, presence of rivals never concerned us again.

We see fear of competition on a rather frequent basis. We chose to address it separately from the fear chapter because we see it as a huge deal for those who focus on it. Just to mention one of the aspects of this phenomenon that amazes us: Some of those folks who are affected by it the most are those who have an athletic background, which is all about competition. It was Will Rogers who said, "I have met men I didn't like, but I never got to know a man I didn't like". We have made it our mission on several occasions to get to know our competition and always to mention that redeeming quality we saw in them to all who brought the person up in conversation. We shall only speak of the good, since who we want to be is a work-in-progress and might always be one. By getting to know an individual, we also discover strengths and weaknesses, which allow us to know that we can win because we have an edge. What is our edge? We have a superior sales system. This exists within our superior sales-driven company. So we are now armed to go forward and beat all comers.

Well, it seems that all we have to do is produce a superior product, a great sales system, and develop a system to present this superior product to all prospective clients. If we don't have a great sales system staffed by capable people, we will not be able to grow our businesses with any certainty or speed anyway.

We must know our competition, and then go out and beat them. Remember just saying those words won't make it so. We have to build something that will allow us to do it. Having a great product is only half the battle. I have to put it into the hands of great marketers and great sales people, operating within a great system.

Carl: He is a real competitor and a follower of basketball coach John Wooden's Pyramid of Success. He boldly plays to his strengths. I had to give him this one.

13. SUCCESS

Noun\ sək'ses

: the accomplishment of an aim or purpose

: a person or thing that achieves desired aims or attains prosperity.

"Success is not final, failure is not fatal: it is the courage to continue that counts." Winston Churchill

Each of us has an idea of what our success will look like. Through a good strategic plan and the actual follow-through on that plan, we will discover approaches to our particular business that work and perhaps some that don't work. In either case, it's working as long as we are flexible enough to know that, when indicators show that we should change our tactics, we actually change our tactics.

We have come to understand that the future we want to see will change as each increment of growth and maturity becomes reality. This understanding is diminished a degree by every day that goes by when we do not make something happen.

We can spend the beginning years of our business juggling all the balls, and this is because of the lack of financial resources and business savvy. So we work on three fronts: doing the business, developing savvy, and building financial resources. So from this point, let's talk about defining success. We strongly suggest taking the time to literally write down what an ideal business future looks like. We urge boldness. What would future business to look like, and how do we fit that vision?

OK, now outline the steps necessary to get there and the last step in a real plan; timeline everything.

It seems that far too often entrepreneurs allow the lack of resources to stand in their way of making the dream come true. We will spend what we have to on facilities and equipment and quite often, if the truth be known, more than we have to. So the question is why we don't make the same financial commitment to personnel. We'll spend $40,000 on a piece of equipment to do the work, orders for which we may not have yet, rather than spend the same $40,000 on a salesperson to generate the work for which we bought the piece of equipment in the first place. We see this over and over again as we work with companies who say they want to create a professional sales effort. Know that growth and perhaps survival will depend on your having a professional sales effort.

The next step or perhaps a parallel step you have to make is to have a plan to lead these newly hired professionals to a place called success. We hope it is becoming abundantly clear that defining the steps necessary to having the success we want will, in fact, show us the path. Develop the understanding that following the path will lead us to the success we desire.

Now let's face the demon, and that is determining what we don't do to find our success, and even deeper, why we don't take the steps that we should.

14. REFLECTION

Noun\ rəˈflekSH(ə)n

: serious thought or consideration.

"Without reflection we go blindly on our way, creating more unintended consequences, and failing to achieve anything useful." Margaret J. Wheatley

We avoid it at all costs sometimes, that reflection we get when we truly look at ourselves. We spend an enormous amount of time avoiding our shortcomings, never truly admitting what we see. We spend time putting on a particular persona that fools ourselves and others into believing we are OK, we got this.

True growth only happens once we sit with ourselves and really admit and become fully aware of what we need to change. Growth is lying in wait for us; it is in our grasp. We must stop long enough to really see (split infinitive) our reality. Push through denial; stop covering it up. A pile of crap with perfume on it is still a pile a crap. We must stop pretending blockages are not there, and begin the tedious process of cleaning up the mess; changing, really changing. We must listen to ourselves and others as they show us where we have left the path, and how to find our way again.

Carl: We all need help. Perhaps the better question is: Does Carl think he needs help?

A mentor, a coach, or someone knowledgeable in the ways of business *and* with knowledge of your particular type of business -- who does not have the emotional attachment to your specific business -- can and will have invaluable insights into the heart of your particular weaknesses, can help you correct these weaknesses, and can help you find freedom and profits. Carl, please take a look around.

True change, true acceptance begins inside us. All that external game only delays our success. The more quickly we accept what is getting in our way, the more quickly we will move forward to achieve our success.

What do you see when you look in the mirror of your current circumstances? If you saw this reflection in someone else, what would you tell her?

We often have great clarity in assessing someone else's reflection. What is it? When we see your own reality really see it; then we can do something about it!

The time is now. You do have this; you have the energy, the ZOOM. We have to stop holding ourselves back.

Take a step forward. Do WHATEVER it takes to move forward.

15. ENERGY

Noun\ ˈenərjē

: the strength and vitality required for sustained physical or mental activity.

"People spend too much time finding other people to blame, too much energy finding excuses for not being what they are capable of being, and not enough energy putting themselves on the line, growing out of the past, and getting on with their lives." J. Michael Straczynski

We need energy and energized people. Energy attracts energy. When we embrace this as a truth, then and only then do we understand that energy has to be a natural characteristic of everyone involved in the leadership of our company. It's another one of those qualities that either exists, or it doesn't.

In leading our efforts, energy and a sense of urgency go hand in hand; it's impossible to have one without the other. This energy saves us money, which again is profit, which is the ultimate scorecard of how we did. We don't mean to suggest it's the only entry on our scorecard, but if profit goes away, everything goes away. OK, does everyone feel pumped up?

In leading our company's efforts, those of us involved need to be aware of new opportunities and threats and take action in a manner that is always present when there is energy. This manner is prudent, calculated, informed, professional, and devoid of procrastinating elements.

When sales is the responsibility we are charged with, we have to understand that all sales success comes from creating edges – advantages, distinctions -- for us and our company, and one of those edges is certainly being the first company to respond to a request, to be the first company to present a proposal. Delivering a proposal in person also flies in the face of today's world, which seems to dictate that all submissions should be transmitted electronically. Well, it is not necessarily true. All accomplished sales people know that the "close" is much more likely to occur when presented in person. So putting some energy here, whenever possible, is the right thing to do.

Production efforts are also better when energy exists within this part of our business. Establishing a sense of urgency, through an understanding that if something is worth doing it is worth doing today, will pay substantial dividends.

So now we must qualify that working with an energy that creates significant action doesn't mean a lack of prudence. Seeking input from other involved parties is always a good idea, so that our communication efforts are intact.

Example: Carl liked to relax and see what developed and then make unilateral decisions. He's no longer in business, and when he was, he experienced constant turnover and significant shrinkage as a result of his efforts or lack thereof.

Get Out of Your Own Way!

It is fear that produces the resistance behavior that keeps us stuck and kills our dreams. It is fear, then, that we need to recognize and eliminate. To get out of your own way, find your ZOOM. Achieve your success. You must get honest with yourself, get out of denial, take a hard look at your shortcomings, and begin to do something, anything differently. Sometimes you need to enlist the help of a consultant or counselor to clean the lenses of your life and business. Often we get so comfortable in our behavioral patterns; we just can't or won't see what is really happening.

We just spend our time in survival mode. We are no longer creating the life we want; we are merely surviving the one we have.

You have to take charge. You have to get up, and do it differently. You have to put your energy into finding resources that can help you see your patterns and break them. You have to put on those new shoes, and starting walking this out. As baseball catcher-philosopher Yogi Berra said, "When you come to a fork in the road, take it."

Change is hard, but change is the only way. The status quo has served its time. Carpe ZOOM. We need to seize our ZOOM. Rekindle the passion that got us started in the first place. Take the energy and applied to surviving, and apply it to thriving.

Be intentional. Make a plan. Brainstorm with another person who isn't close to you or your business, who has a different perspective or vantage point of you and your business. Get it all out on paper, clearly visible to you. Then get out of your own way, get at it, and get what you want.

The time is now, not tomorrow. Not when a certain employee retires, because you are afraid to let her go, even though she is toxic for your business. Not when you have the finances.

Not when you get more education, not in a month, or after the next big sale. Not when your personal life settles down or any other number of excuses. What is it that is holding you back? See it, accept it, and do something about it. Find your ZOOM again.

ZOOM is a verb. ZOOM is action! ZOOM is knowing what you need to do and then doing it.

And so, what are we to make of all that's been discussed? Where should all these thoughts lead us?

We firmly believe that once we really decide we want to progress, we then need to determine where the changes need to be and exactly how that progresses. What we mean by that is: There needs to be a plan formulated with a timeline to assure that there will be results and not just endless talk of results. Then we have to fill in our existing weaknesses. It would probably be a good idea to fill in these weaknesses before we start to plan. Fear is now turning into courage, the minute we realize that change will happen within us; the minute we decide we're going to pursue it and start to formulate the plan. Not the minute we start to talk about it. We've probably already talked it to death. So if we are willing to accept our weaknesses and not take them on, then we are done.

In business when we analyze strengths and weaknesses, we can often hire someone to bridge our weaknesses. For example, if we don't have a good sales record and realize that sales are not a current strength, we can hire that strength. The strengths and weaknesses we are talking about here are fundamental to successful leadership, so leaders have no choice but to develop these traits in employees if they are not present. What happens next?

ZOOM

verb \ˈzüm

: to move quickly

: to move quickly upward

: to increase suddenly

Who Are We?

We all have roles to play in our businesses. So what's your role, and do you play it well? Often in small business we play several roles, and some of these roles are a real chore for us. That is, they're not what we want to do or are called to do, but we do them anyway.

The only way really to get past the above situation is to grow our company to the point where we can see our way clear to have the key people in place who can finally allow us to fill the role that we are good at and passionate about. So once again we have to generate revenue through productive, professional sales and marketing efforts that will allow us to assume the full-time role of entrepreneur. We will need staff who know how to do this. Come on, it's just another business investment. Let the fear go. If you do it right, you'll be very happy.

So who are the classic entrepreneurs? They are visionaries, dreamers, and starters. What they are typically not is doers or finishers. It all starts with the dreamer and progresses through the doer (production) to the finisher (salesperson). Be that successful visionary, and take your place in the organization. Simply pay attention to all of it for an hour each day, and be the dreamer. If you just can't manage that, hire a general manager. Move forward, and make wise decisions on who joins your team. If you're in doubt about that, hire a coach and/or consultant to help you, but move forward NOW.

www.ingramcontent.com/pod-product-compliance
Lightning Source LLC
Chambersburg PA
CBHW060617210326
41520CB00010B/1379